Contents

INTRODUCTION

A garden pond, or a water garden as it is often called, adds enormous appeal to a garden. It can be large or small, simple or dramatic. It can include waterfalls, fountains, elaborate rockwork, and special lighting, or it can be serenely empty. It can be a natural pond with a flowing spring or a plastic tub.

Choose your garden pond while considering the size of your property, the amount of maintenance you wish to do, your budget, and the style of your garden.

Many homeowners make a garden pond using prefabricated parts from a garden center or home improvement store. Others are more free-form in their design. The container for your pond can be a commercial preformed tub designed for the purpose, a freeform hole dug and lined by the maker, or even an old bathtub! For a small pond, a capacity of about 20 gallons is a practical size. Water weighs about eight pounds per gallon, so if your pond is elevated, be sure the supports can hold that much weight. Black, charcoal, and dark green colors are good choices, since they give an impression of greater depth and discourage algae growth.

Placement Of A Garden Pond

Placing the pond is very important. As with a fountain, consider what location will give you the greatest pleasure. Remember that children and pets love standing water, so consider their safety as well. Placing the pond in an open area will reduce the time you spend clearing fallen leaves and other debris out of the water. Sunlight is very important. Most aquatic plants need six to eight hours of direct sunlight daily to grow well.

Water

If you want your aquatic plants to be healthy, filling the container with clean water is essential. Don't use water that has been altered by a water softener. City water is normally treated with chlorine and may contain other additives as well. Let the water sit in the tub for at least 24 hours before adding plants, so that the chlorine can evaporate. If your community uses chloramine, a more stable form of chlorine, you will need to use a commercial product to decontaminate the water.

A Small Ecosystem

A water garden is a miniature ecosystem that must be in balance to remain healthy. Typically, it takes three or four weeks for a new garden pond to establish a healthy balance. About two weeks after it is set up, the water normally turns cloudy with algae. A week or so later, the aquatic plants will get the algae under control by absorbing sunlight and nutrients that contribute to algae growth. Then the water will clear. It will remain clear as long as the ecosystem is in balance.

Plants

Plants grown in artificial garden ponds are rooted in individual pots, which are placed in the water-filled pond container. You can use a soil mixture specially made for water gardening or just a very heavy clay garden soil as a potting medium. Topping the pot with half an inch of pea gravel helps to keep the soil in place.

Many aquatic plants have very specific preferences for the depth of water they prefer. You can put bricks beneath the pots to bring the plant to its preferred depth.

For maximum health of your pond, only about half the water surface should be covered with plants. Aquatic plants are usually divided into three categories: floating, emergent or marginal, and submerged. Both floating and submerged plants are needed for a healthy pond ecosystem.

Marginal Plants

Emergent plants are often called marginals because in nature they are found along the margins of ponds. They grow at the muddy edges, often with their roots and part of their stems underwater, while their leaves and flowers are above water. Bog plants are also considered marginals, and many of them will grow in areas that have limited sunlight. Some tolerate as little as three hours of sunlight a day. Consider some of these emergent plants for your water garden:

- Sagittaria - Arrowheads
- Iris versicolor - Blue Flag
- Cyperus isocladus - Dwarf Papyrus
- Ruellia brittoniana - Water Blue Bells
- Juncus effusus - Corkscrew Rush
- Lotus
- Water Lilies

Submerged Plants

These plants, sometimes called oxygenators, grow largely or entirely beneath the surface of the water. They produce oxygen, reduce algae by consuming nutrients, and provide cover for fish. They are often potted in gravel, because their roots are used only to anchor them to the bottom of the pond. A healthy pond should have one bunch of submerged plants for every two square feet of surface water. Good submerged plants for a small pond include:

- Vallisneria - Wild Celery
- Cabomba canadensis - Fanwort
- Egeria densa - Anacharis

Floating Plants

Floaters are not rooted in the soil. They float freely just above or just below the water surface. Some gardeners like to use a framework to restrict them to specific parts of the pond, while others allow them to be pushed by breezes and water movement to any area. Some floaters reproduce rapidly. Excess plants should be scooped from the water occasionally. Popular floating plants include:

- Salvinia longifolia - Giant Velvet Leaf
- Eichhornia crassipes - Water Hyacinth
- Pistia stratiotes - Water Lettuce
- Algae Problems
- water garden with fountain

A balanced ecosystem will have few problems with algae growth. Most problems are caused by overfeeding fish, over fertilizing plants, or having too few plants available to take up the nutrients in the pond.

Reducing available nutrients is the best way to eliminate algae problems. The most obvious method is to reduce the fish food and fertilizer added to the pond. It may be necessary to flush the pond and add fresh water. Adding more aquatic plants, until about 50 per cent of the water surface is covered, is also useful. Larger ponds may require a pump and filter system.

A common algae problem that pond owners face is the dreaded string algae. It begins to appear once the sun is brightly shining on your pond. Especially in the spring before the plants have begun to spring up after their winter dormant period. String algae actally battles with your aquatic plants for nutrients that are floating in the pond.

At this point your balanced ecosystem becomes messed up with mounds of stringy algae that is quickly taking over. You may need help to elimate it if you cannot take care of it on your own.

The most balanced ecosystems may need help sometimes. You may need a supplement that breaks down organic materials that are creating problems around waterfalls, rocks, planted pots and filtration systems. It can help to spot treat the most troubled areas of your pond. You can follow up company with their product S.A.B. for a full attack on string algae.

These products do not contain chemicals, which make them safe for your pond life. If you don't go this route you may prefer to get in the pond and weed the string algae out by hand or with a toilet brush taped on a long broom handle.

One other method to think of as an algae control method is barley. Barley straw placed in the pond water decomposes which then releases a chemical. Barley breakdown combined with water and sunlight begins to form a certain peroxide which breaks down the cell walls of the algae. Barley pellets may be purchased to be used inside most filters and skimmer systems. You may even set them along the inside of the pond using a mesh bag for easy application.

If you begin to get that dreaded green water during the hot summer months, beneficial bacteria can save the pond. Beneficial bacteria added according to the directions on the bottle is an important thing to do to maintain clear and healthy balanced pond water. You may try other products to supply the good bacteria to the pond. Both the liquid and dry forms are chemical free and 100% all-natural.

Use chemical applications only as a last resort, since many can injure plants and animals. Follow directions very carefully and employ proper safety precautions. It is essential to not go overboard when treating your pond. Contact your local water garden supplier if you need guidance. Let nature take care of your pond's health when you can. An established pond (a few years old) usually needs less care than a brand new one, as the natural, balanced ecosystem has now taken over the perfect care of your beautiful pond.

Winter

Unless you live in a subtropical or tropical climate, plants in a small garden pond will have to be moved indoors for the winter. Plants can be moved while still in their pots to water-filled tubs placed in a cool, dark basement. The plants will go dormant for the winter and revive when they are placed back in the garden the following spring. Floaters can be over-wintered in aquariums under bright light.

Garden Pond Building Tips

A garden pond adds beauty, elegance, and lively interest to a yard. Whether a fish pond, a receiving basin for a waterfall, or simply a placid body of water for meditation and reflection, a garden pond provides a focal point that enhances nearly all yards.

But to successfully create a garden pond that looks natural, it helps to follow a few basic guidelines to make the building go smoother, and for easier continued maintenance of the pond.

Level the Garden Pond Perimeter to Close Tolerances

When digging the hole for the garden pond, remember that a garden pond's water level is only as high as the lowest point of the pond perimeter. In other words, the entire perimeter of the garden pond needs to be as near to the same height as possible.

This might be a point that seems obvious from afar, but when you are digging the pond it can often escape attention. Since an exact level is not possible, think in terms of deviation and tolerances. For example, if your chosen pond depth is 24 inches, the perimeter's deviation from that height should be as little as possible: just an inch or two.

Decide Whether the Pond Will Be Shallow or Deep

The depth of the garden pond is an important decision that affects both cost and the eventual appearance of the pond. As the pond gets deeper, the bottom becomes less visible and rock cannot be seen. Fish might tuck themselves away, hidden. Deeper ponds also require the use of additional expensive pond liner. Shallow ponds are better for displaying decorative rocks on the bottom and fish are more prominent. But shallow ponds tend to build up algae faster because the light can reach more of the water with greater intensity.

Protect the Pond Bottom Against Burrowing Animals

Burrowing pests such as groundhogs and moles can dig up holes in a lawn and garden. When you have a burrowing animal in your yard, it seems like you're always filling in holes. But the problem goes well past the point of annoying when the burrowing animal exits under your garden pond, chewing away pond liner in the process. The solution is to lay down a metal mesh called hardware cloth as a base for your pond bottom before shoveling a few inches of dirt over it. Then underlayment and liner go on top of the dirt layer. If your sides are dirt, not retaining wall block, then you should lay hardware cloth on the sides, too.

Reconcile Eventual Pond Size With the Pond Liner Size

A garden pond can only be as large as the size of its underlying pond liner. So, you have some questions to answer before shovel meets dirt. Quality pond liners made of ethylene propylene diene terpolymer (EPDM) are very expensive, while PVC liners are expensive but less so than EPDM. In a project that involves the use of free or low-cost materials such as rock, concrete slabs, retaining wall blocks, and the lowest cost item of all, water, spending hundreds of dollars for a sheet of the liner can be a daunting prospect. If your budget is tight, then the cost of the pond liner will always dictate the size of the pond. On the other hand, you might find that it is worthwhile to put a little extra money into a high-visibility, curb appeal project such as this.

Early Shape Nuances Are Often Lost

When you initially create the shape of the pond, you may find yourself adding special curves and inlets that you feel will give the garden pond a unique look. But these early delicate nuances often get softened and obliterated with each subsequent stage of the pond-building process. Adding underlayment, liner, rocks at the bottom of the pond, and especially rocks along the bank of the pond all contribute to this softening process. Think in terms of basic shapes.

Add a Top Spillover Drain in the Design

Unless you live in a parched, arid climate, your pond will inevitably overflow. Yet even in dry areas, this can happen when you are filling with the hose and let the time slip away. Rather than having the pond spill over and race toward your house foundation, create a predictable spillover point so that water can go to a safe spot.

Avoid Tall, Vertical Garden Pond Walls

The more vertical and tall the walls of the garden pond, the harder the job you will have when you apply stone to the pond. Loose, natural stones are difficult to stack vertically. Not only does the rock tend to fall, but a greater amount of rocks or larger rocks are also needed to cover this area. Small rocks are less expensive but hard to stack. Large rocks cover vertical spaces easier but are costly and difficult to move. Try to keep the garden pond banks at a 45-degree angle or less, if possible.

Install a Permanent External Water Filter and Skimmer

Unless you make provisions for a permanent water filter mounted in your pond's wall, your only options for filtration will be manual skimming or floating filtration devices. Hand skimming is a constant job while floating filters take up a lot of water surface and are unsightly. A permanent water filter mounted on the side of the pond stays out of the way. Since it is automatic, it will turn on at set intervals. While a permanent filter is more difficult and costly to install at first, it makes for easier pond maintenance over the long term.

Terrace the Pond Bottom

Sloped garden pond banks, if angled sharply enough, result in sliding rock at the bottom and sides of the pond.

Instead, terrace the garden pond's sides and bottom, much like farming terraces or stair risers and treads. Keep each terrace riser no more than about 6 inches high to avoid stacking rocks too high. Create terraces by cutting them directly in the dirt with the shovel, as long as the dirt is packed tight enough to hold shape.

Plan in Advance for Covering the Pond Liner

Every single square inch of pond liner must be covered up. Even the best, most expensive pond liner is subject to the sun's punishing UV rays and will break down. The way to protect against deterioration is by covering up all of the liner with something permanent, like rocks up the sides, river pebbles, or smooth gravel on the bottom. It's better to think ahead about how you want to cover up the liner. Doing so in hindsight often means overloading the pond liner. For example, if you keep the pond terraces low enough, you can use smaller rocks. High terraces demand larger, more visually intrusive fill items.

Be Inventive About Sourcing Your Rocks

Garden ponds require a lot of rocks on the bottom and the sides to cover up the liner. If you were to purchase all of the rocks, the cost of the pond would increase substantially. Instead, look around for rocks that you can use whenever you are out. When you go on a trip and find a legitimate source of rock, toss a few in your car. Rivers are a good source for rounded river stones. Beaches, too, provide an endless source of pebbles, round stones, and sand. Just make sure that you can legally take the stones.

Think Ahead to Cleaning

One of the more dreaded aspects of owning a garden pond is cleaning it. Garden ponds collect leaves, dust, dirt, and all sorts of debris. Eventually, you need to empty out the pond and clean it. One way to make cleaning day easier is to create a pond bottom that is smoother and easier to clean. Heavily rocked pond bottoms and those that are heavily textured are more difficult to clean. Lay down only as much rock as is needed to cover the pond liner.

Use an EPDM Liner If Possible

Even though PVC pond liners are vastly cheaper than EPDM liners, EPDM liners are usually worth purchasing, if you can afford it. EPDM liners are thicker and far more durable than PVC liners. They resist UV rays well, and even chemicals such as chlorine are no match for EPDM. Also, when warmed by the sun, EPDM liners become pliable and fit well into the pond hole.

How to Build a Garden Pond Using Retaining Wall Blocks

Building a landscape pond is a great way to improve the value of your property. It's also fairly simple, although the work does involve a fair amount of manual labor. The good news is that whenever you are performing your own labor rather than hiring others to do it, the potential for saving money is substantial. A DIY pond is generally half the cost of a professionally installed pond of equal size.

There are two primary methods for building a landscape pond: using a hard plastic liner shell or using a flexible liner. Flexible liners have advantages since they allow you to build a pond of whatever shape and size you want. In ideal circumstances, building a pond with a flexible liner is a matter of excavating a hole, cutting the flexible liner to size and installing it, then securing the edges with landscape stone and filling the pond with water. While the work can involve plenty of labor digging, prying, cutting roots, and more it is not very complicated and almost anyone in good health can do it.

But the project becomes more complicated if your conditions are not ideal. When your building site has loose, sandy soil, for example, the walls of your pond won't hold their shape and may collapse when people walk around the edges. The solution is to use concrete retaining wall blocks to shore up the sides of the excavation before the flexible liner is installed.

Choosing a Flexible Liner

Building a pond is not extravagantly expensive since most of the materials are relatively economical. But don't try to save money by buying a cheap liner, since this is the most important element. Flexible pond liners are generally made of one of two flexible materials: PVC or EPDM (ethylene propylene diene, a synthetic rubber). PVC liners are best suited for smaller ponds, while EPDM is a better choice for larger ponds. The liners are typically sold in sheets 12 x 15 feet or larger, which you will need to cut down to fit the shape and size of your pond. For very large ponds, it is possible to join two or more sheets together, using the same taping/patching materials used to repair a pond.

Better liners will use thicker EPDM rubber a 45 mil product is recommended. PVC liners are typically thinner, but make sure to choose a product with a thickness of at least 30 ml.

Check with your permitting and planning departments to see if building permits are required or if there are zoning restrictions. In some areas, protective fencing may be required around a yard with a pond. Before you begin digging, call your local utility locator service. This free service will help you avoid gas, electrical, water, and other vital services when you dig.

Pick a dry time of year for this project, since excavation will be easiest in dry, loose soil. Work at times of the day when you have the most energy. Wear well-worn work clothes, as this is very dirty work and you may want to discard the clothes when finished.

Allow plenty of time for the project. Depending on the size of the pond, it may well take you a month or more from the moment your shovel first contacts earth to the moment you turn on the hose to fill the pond

What You'll Need

- Equipment / Tools
- Garden hose

- Shovel or spade
- Laser level
- Long rope
- Tape measure
- Utility knife or shears

Materials

- Powdered chalk or flour
- Concrete building blocks
- Retaining wall blocks
- Hardware cloth (if needed)
- Pond underlayment
- Pond liner
- Natural stones
- River gravel or small smooth stone

Instructions

Lay Out the Pond Boundary

Start by outlining the pond site on the ground. The classic way to mark pond boundaries is with a garden hose because it naturally forms wide, gradual curves. If you wish, you can now sprinkle flour or chalk around the hose to mark the edges of the pond.

It's a fairly common mistake to undersize a landscape pond. Most experts recommend that a healthy, balanced pond with plants and fish should be a minimum of 50 square feet (a surface area of 10 x 5 feet, or an 8-foot diameter, if the pond is circular). The depth of a standard landscape pond should be 18 to 24 inches, although depths up to 32 inches are possible with very large ponds.

Dig Out the Pond Border

Next, dig out the pond border. Make shovel-width cuts in the grass or dirt, following the boundary outline. For grass sod, it helps to use a spade which allows for narrower cuts. Slide the spade under the segmented turf to remove it. With the edges of the pond clearly marked, you can remove the hose.

Excavate the Center of Pond

After the pond perimeter is established, the long work of excavating the earth begins. First, remove all dirt within the boundaries of the pond, down to the same depth that the border strip was excavated.

Next, excavate down to the lowest point in your pond, wherever that that might be located (normally it is near the center of the pond). This helps you establish a base-line for your pond's depth. No other part of the pond bottom should be excavated deeper than this point. From the center, you can now begin excavating outward to the sides. Begin by digging out the entire area that will form the deepest bottom tier of the pond.

Create Tiers

As your excavation moves outward the sides of the pond, create flat-bottomed tiers, with each tier about 8 inches higher than the previous one. Concrete building blocks with 8-inch sides make perfect boundaries for these tiers. A perimeter of concrete blocks at each level will serve as a retaining wall to hold back the soil of the next higher tier of the pond.

The goal is for your pond to "step up" as it approaches the sides. A large pond with a 24-inch center depth can have as many as three tiers, each bounded with a perimeter of 8-inch tall concrete blocks; smaller ponds may require just two. Keep the walls of the tiers relatively short, since this will simplify the later step of covering the blocks with rocks. By keeping the height of the tiers short, you can span the vertical distance with one or two rocks.

Reinforce With Retaining Wall Blocks

As you approach the edges of the pond, reinforce the perimeter of the last tier with retaining wall blocks laid over the concrete blocks. This is especially important where the building site has sandy, loose soil these blocks help retain the pond's shape and height. Small retaining wall blocks give you better flexibility and are easier to work with.

Check for Level Frequently

A laser level is a highly valuable tool when building a pond. If you own a bubble level only, or no level at all, you should purchase a laser level, if only for this one project.

It's quite critical to check the tiers and edges of the pond frequently to make sure they remain level and flat. A pond that is slightly off-kilter can't be filled to a uniform water level.

Lay Hardware Cloth

If your yard has burrowing animals, such as groundhogs or moles, eventually they may find your pond and burrow upwards, piercing your expensive liner. To protect against this, purchase rolls of hardware cloth (1/4-inch grid) and lay it out over the entire pond bottom. Then spread about at least 2 inches of dirt over the hardware cloth to cushion it.

Measure for the Liner

Pond liners are expensive, so it makes sense to wait until the excavation is complete to measure and buy a liner to fit the pond. The easiest way to do this is to use a rope to measure the pond in both directions. Begin by placing one end of the rope about 2 feet beyond the edge of the pond, then run the rope down into the pond, flush against the bottom of each tier, and up the other side of the pond, ending about 2 feet beyond the far edge. Use a tape measure to measure the rope to determine this dimension for the liner.

Take similar measurements for the perpendicular dimension of the pond. Unless your pond is irregularly shaped, these length and width measurements are all you need to buy a pond liner sufficient to cover your pond.

Install the Pond Underlayment

Before installing the liner, lay down an underlayment to cushion and protect the liner from roots, rocks, and other objects that may damage it. Specialty pond underlayment is available from landscape supply stores, or you can use pieces of old carpeting.

Install the Pond Liner

With a helper, lay the folded liner across the pond bottom. Then, unfold it so that it drapes over the sides of the pond. Be patient with this step as you slowly and painstakingly press the liner down onto the pond bottom, creating folded pleats. While the bottom may have just a few pleats, all of the sides will be pleated. Con't worry about the pleats and wrinkles in the liner; they will hidden by later steps.

Trim down the edges of the liner so that no more than 1 to 2 feet of liner overhangs the side of the pond. Secure the edges of the pond liner with stones to hold it in place.

Add Rock to the Pond Walls

Cover side walls of the pond and each tier wall with natural stone. Start with large and medium-sized rocks, building up the sides until no pond liner is visible. After the walls are entirely covered, use small stones or smooth river pebbles to cover the entire bottom of the pond.

Fill With Water

Fill your pond with a garden hose. It will take several hours to fill the pond to its maximum level. If you are adding plants or fish, make sure to follow recommended practice for the types of fish and plants you are using. This can include allowing the water to stabilize for a period of time and/or adding chemicals or filtering equipment.

How to Build A Garden Pond

Before you begin you will need the following things:

- shovel
- trowel
- garden hose

- plank of wood
- spirit level
- pond liner
- sand/liner underlay/newspaper
- bricks
- landscaping rocks
- fountain pump
- [optional] black vinyl duct tape
- [optional] cement & bucket

Step 1: Digging the Hole

First dig yourself a good hole. I had a look at pond liners that were available first and knew that I could get one that is 2.5x2m for $39, so that meant that I wanted to keep my pond less than 1.5x1m and no more than 50cm deep. You can use a garden hose as a guide to work out your approximate shape.

You want to dig the sides straight down, but be careful that you don't break off parts of the wall as we want them nice and solid for later. You might want to start a little smaller than your ideal size and make it bigger as you go just incase you do accidentally collapse part of a wall. One point to realise is that once you have put on the rocks at the end it will seem smaller so don't be afraid if it looks really big right now.

Take off the crumbly top soil to a width of 4-5 inches around the hole if this is an issue for you like it is for me. The top soil for us was only about an inch thick, which gives us a solid foundation for the bricks. Use a straight plank of wood and a spirit level to make sure your sides are reasonably in line across the pond. Use a hand trowel to shave off a little more if some areas are higher than others.

Create a deep part and a shallow part in your pond. The centre of my hole is about 15cm deeper than the small area at the top. This will allow us to put in a range of plants as we desire. Some plants can only be placed in up to 20cm of water, some like it a lot deeper. Think about the fish you are going to get when you are planning your size as well as Koi need a much deeper, larger area than other fish.

Check for rocks and roots that may puncture your liner. After scraping with the shovel and removing most of the rocks I used my hands to feel around all the areas of the pond and dug out any more small rocks with the trowel.

Next, place your underlay in the hole. I used about an inch of sand in the bottom and on the ledge. You can also use damp newspaper, carpet or special underlay that you can buy from garden centres.

Step 2: Lay the Liner in the Hole

Lay your liner over the hole. Try not to drag the liner around too much, but with a little draping and patience, you can achieve a neat look with your liner. I took off my shoes and spent some time pushing it gently into all the corners and doing some initial pleating. You may want to use some black vinyl duct tape to tape down some of the pleats like I did to make them even less noticeable. Use bricks or stones to hold the liner down neatly all around the pond.

Step 3: Put in Some Water

This is the step that most instructions jump straight to, though after my first attempt I took the extra time at step 2. Start to fill the pond with water until it is about half full (or 2 inches from the top of the liner). You can see here that I filled it about half way up to the bottom of the bricks. As it is filling you can gently ease out the liner at any areas where you need to allow more liner to reach the bottom or fix up any pleats.

When you are happy with the liner (take your time and get it right!) place your layer of bricks around the ledge. The purpose of the bricks is so that you will be able to have the water level above the liner so you will not notice it is there. There is nothing more distracting from a pond than seeing the ugly creases in a black plastic pond liner as per our first try, dubbed "Fail Pond".

Step 4: Secure the Liner

If you are planning on having a pump or water feature, you will want to think about its placement and where the power cables and any other hoses will go at this point. We decided to have a simple water feature, so I placed the pump in the desired position and ran the cord to the side of the pond. I did not run the cord to the back because you don't want to be looking at the cord when you are standing in front of the pond. The cord runs to the bottom below and then around the bricks until it comes out the back where you can see the cable as this is the closest point to the house. Test the water feature! It is better to ensure it works now than have to take half of the pond apart to get it back out!

An optional step at this point is to fill any gaps between the bricks with quick setting cement. I used this between each brick so that any dirt or sand packed behind would be less likely to run into the pond when it is full of water. You do not need to make it waterproof as the pond liner takes care of this. Allow your cement to cure for 3-4 hours before proceeding.

Next gently ease the liner straight up behind the bricks and pack dirt up to it like a ramp, then fold the liner down and pack dirt over top. The liner comes up to the level of the bricks and then is hidden and slopes away from the pond. This should mean I won't get a run off (including dirt) flowing into the pond, and any overflow will flow away from it.

Note also that we decided to have a "wetland" area for our pond. At the top of the photo there is a semi-circle of sand where the liner continues flat at the level of the bottom of the bricks under the sand, and then is built up in a mound. The sand area will be constantly wet allowing us to grow plants that like wet feet, but do not like to be submerged. You could do this too, or skip this part for a simple pond.

Step 5: Position Rocks

Gently ease your rocks onto the sides and where possible, allow them to overlap the bricks completely. This step allows complete coverage of the pond liner and is the decorative part of the pond. It is handy to have a number of rocks to choose from so you can play with their positioning until you are happy with how it looks.

Fill the pond up to the bottom of the bricks.

Step 6: Final Touches

Waiting 24 hours gives the cement a chance to cure and your bricks and rocks a chance to settle into place. Top up the wetland with more sand as the rocks will hold that in place. Now it is time to fill up the pond until 1-2cm below the top of the bricks and add your plants. Wait at least 2 days before adding fish, or follow the recommendations from your local aquarium expert.

Budget Friendly DIY Garden Ponds You Can Make This Weekend

With warmer weather comes my itch to get outdoors and spruce up my gardens. I love nothing more than spending an afternoon in the flower garden, pruning back dead leaves or planting new blooms. With that in mind, I thought about adding some water features this year. I love a good water feature. To me, there is nothing more relaxing than sitting by a body of water and just lazing the day away. So, I started looking for some DIY garden ponds to add to my flower garden. I found 15 of the most amazing DIY garden ponds that are so cheap and easy to build that you are definitely going to want to put in one of these this spring.

I love cheap and easy. Anything that fits into my budget is a winner in my book and all of these DIY garden ponds are low cost to build and to maintain. If you really want to add some decorative features to your flower gardens, you just have to take a look at some of these. From upcycled tires to outright digging it yourself, you have so many options with regards to how you can build your garden pond. And, these DIY versions are so much less expensive than having one put in by a landscaping company.

- DIY Backyard Pond

You can build your own backyard pond in a weekend with the right tools and supplies. This one uses patio pavers or rocks as well as a traditional pond liner, all of which you can get at your local home improvement store. Your actual cost will depend on the materials and tools that you already have on hand but you can make this one really budget friendly if you have a few bricks or patio pavers that you can repurpose.

- Repurposed Plastic Storage Tote Garden Pond

You don't have to spend a fortune on a premade backyard pond form. You can simply turn an old Rubbermaid plastic container into your garden pond and save that money for other things. This one is really easy and if you have a rather large plastic tote that you can use, it is also really cheap to build. Add a fountain, some river rock and something for the edges and you have a gorgeous garden pond on the cheap.

- Lighted Zen Container Pond

This container pond is perfect for placing on your patio. It is a really easy one to set up and you add a light so it is the perfect garden pond for relaxing beside on those warm spring and summer evenings. You just need a large container and a few other supplies to make this one and it's a pretty cheap garden pond to build. A relaxing DIY Zen garden is the perfect addition to any backyard.

- DIY Bubble Container Pond

Here is another beautiful container pond that is perfect for adding a bit of unique style to your garden. You need a couple of containers for this one and you can pick up rather cheap ones. The fountain bubbles above the pond, giving it the perfect relaxing sound. You can easily have this one completed in an afternoon.

- DIY Paver Pond With Fountain

Those patio pavers or river rocks are perfect for creating this DIY garden pond that has a handmade rock fountain at the top. This would be beautiful in the center of your flower garden or you could place it anywhere that you want to add a bit of style and design. Add some water lilies when you're finished and it's a beautiful addition to any landscaping. A DIY Paver fountain is a beautiful way to decorate your outdoors.

- Repurposed Stock Tank Garden Pond

To make a garden pond, you simply need something that will hold water. An old stock tank makes a wonderful choice. This one is so easy that you can have it set up in just a couple of hours. You can bury the tank so that it is ground level or just level it up and add water. Add some rocks and plants around it and you'll have a quick and easy garden pond that costs just a fraction of one that is professionally designed.

- River Rock Covered Pond

If you happen to have a garden pond form you can pick these up at home improvement stores and they aren't that expensive you can build a gorgeous custom garden pond by just inserting the form into the ground and adding some beautiful river rock or slate. River rock can be found in so many places and if you are lucky enough to have it near your home, you can often get it for free.

- Low Budget Waterfall Pond

Those rocks that you pick up out of your yard make the perfect base for a gorgeous garden pond. This one has a lovely waterfall, that you also create from rock. If you happen to have a lot of rock on your property, you can build this one for just the cost of the liner and pump. If you don't have any rock to use, check with friends and neighbors. Chances are that they will gladly give it to you if you simply remove it from their yards.

- DIY Recycled Tractor Tire Pond

If you have an old tractor tire, you can use that to create a lovely outdoor pond. This one is really easy to build and if you have the tire on hand, it doesn't cost much at all to get it up and running. There are so many things that you can do with an old tractor tire. Recycled tire DIY projects are wonderful and they help you to reuse those old tires and keep them out of the landfill. There are so many beautiful ways to upcycle old tires.

- DIY Ecological Liner-Less Natural Garden Pond

If you want something really simple and really ecological, this liner-less natural garden pond is it. You don't need any sort of liner, which makes the setup much easier than most garden ponds. Bentonite clay acts as the liner to keep water from being absorbed into the ground. This one is really gorgeous when it is finished and you can build it for just the cost of the clay, which isn't much.

- Easy DIY Garden Fish Pond

If you want to add goldfish or Koi to your garden pond, this is a great one to build. It is so easy you just dig it out, add your liner, and then choose the rocks and other decorations that you want to add. This is great for keeping those little fish and you could easily add a waterfall feature as well if you want. Just be careful to block the pump with mesh to keep your fish from being sucked into the waterfall.

- DIY Rectangular Pond With Wooden Deck

Some old pallets can be recycled to make the deck for this modern rectangular pond. I love DIY pallet projects.

Or, you can use any boards that you have on hand that are left over from other projects. The pond itself is really easy to build and it is perfect if you are looking for something a bit more modern and contemporary than traditional round ponds. This would also be perfect if you wanted to add a few goldfish or Koi.

- DIY Multi Basin Recycled Tire Pond

This tire pond is not just one tire, it is several. You can use tires of different sizes to create different basins and give your garden pond a really unique and natural look. You just need a collection of old used tires and a few rocks, as well as your liner and there are many options for a liner that are cheaper than a traditional pond liner. Just design your pond with as many basins as you have tires available.

- DIY Pond And Stream With Waterfall

If you have the outdoor space available, this DIY pond and stream would be beautiful in your garden area or backyard. You can make the stream go as far as you want it to go and the waterfall is absolutely gorgeous at the end of it. This one really isn't as complicated to build as it looks and it really does look like a natural stream when you get it finished.

- Simple Preformed Garden Pond

If all else fails and you just don't have the time or the inclination to dig the pond yourself, you can buy a preformed garden pond and just drop it into the ground. The trick with this one is to find the perfect shape for the look that you are trying to achieve and to lay out your rocks to make it look gorgeous. It's simple and you can have this one finished in just an afternoon.

Pond Types

There are many pond types, kinds and sizes. Each of them has its unique characteristics. Before you start laying a pond it is important that you make a choice of different types of ponds. There are different kinds of ponds you can choose from. You may choose for example kinds of ponds, including:

- Biological pond
- Fish pond
- Koi pond
- Mini pond
- Mirror pond
- Natural pond
- Ornamental pond
- Plant pond
- Swimming pond
- Terrace pond
- Wildlife pond
- Koi pond

If we talk about a Koi pond, it is about a pond with koi, the national fish of Japan. A koi is a special domesticated version of common carp. They are beautiful fish to look at. Koi need a duly maintained pond to guarantee health of these valuable fish. The technique applied in koi ponds should therefore be inspected and maintained regularly.

Minipond

Een mini vijver of mini pond is een kleine draagbare decoratieve vijver die geschikt is voor de kleinste tuinen, terrassen en balkonsA mini-pond is a small portable decorative pond basin. A mini-pond is suitable for the smallest gardens, terraces and balconies. If you dispose of somewhat more space, put several mini-ponds side by side. In different colours, for example.

Wildlife pond

In a wildlife pond nature is in charge. The number of plants is rich and the water attracts many animals, such as frogs, salamanders and insects. In a wildlife pond no pump, filter, chemical means and in ideal conditions also no liner is used. A proper number and variety of (oxygen) plants affords a high level oxygen content in the water, securing it from algae.

Fish pond

A fish pond is a pond which is merely meant to keep fish. The consequence of total admittance of plants in a fish pond is that more efforts have to be made to keep the water clear and healthy, because there are no plants to filter the water, whereas fish still produce waste material.

Swimming pond

You want to lay a beautiful pond, however, your children want to take a nice dip in the swimming pool in the garden. The ideal solution will be then a beautiful swimming pond from which everyone can get a great deal of pleasure.

If you have decided what kind of pond you are going to build, proper determination of its size and place to build in your garden will be the next step. Pay special attention to the position in relation to any buildings and plantings in regard of shadow, continued growth of roots and foundation.

Besides you should consider what pond form would best fit in with the house and the garden. A stark pond, for example square, L-form or fully round will properly fit in with a modern house and garden. A naturally formed pond, for example, is kidney-shaped.

How To Design A Garden Around A Pond

People typically have ponds in their yards because they like to keep fish and frogs in them, and because they want to attract beautiful butterflies and birds. The ponds are often not very large, but nevertheless add some very nice scenery to the garden. When you plan the landscape design around your pond, make sure that it will provide the natural habitat for the birds, frogs and other animals that will be attracted to the pond. Here are some things you should know and consider when designing a garden around a pond.

- Have the garden around the pond look as natural as possible. Plant flowers and trees that will complement the surroundings of the pond.

- Plant plants between the rocks of the pond, as well as around the pond.
- Plant moss-type plants as well as creeping plants around the pond. These will grow over the rocks.
- Take care not to plant trees or shrubs that will grow too high right next to the pond. You don't want to detract from the impact of the pond. Rather, plant small plants near the pond that will contrast with any vegetation on the water, as well as with the water's greenish color.
- Don't block the view of the pond from your house. It's a good idea to plant shrubs and small trees as a background to your view of the pond from your house.
- Hide your pond's filter or pump by planting shrubs around it

The Pros And Cons Of Garden Ponds

Garden ponds can really divide opinion they are as loved by some as they are loathed by others. There are certainly some pluses and minuses to consider before going ahead and adding a pond to your garden.

A water feature

There's no doubt that the human race, on the whole, loves water. Our towns, cities and resorts are by and large located by the coast, on the banks of a river or close to a lake. The sound and sight of water calms the senses and instils a sense of wellbeing.

A safety issue

If you have small children either resident or as frequent or occasional visitors a pond may pose a safety risk. Will you truly relax in your Outback reclining chairs if you're worried about little ones getting too close to the pond?

Birdlife

One of the joys of pond life is the feathered friends who may come to visit in search of food. You might catch an occasional glimpse or even regular sighting of a colourful, elusive kingfisher, or an elegant, majestic heron.

Fishing

Imagine investing in some beautiful (and pricey) koi carp for your pond, only for them to be swept away pronto by the sharp beak of that grey heron?

High maintenance

It's not simply a case of installing a pre-formed pond or liner, filling it, and that's it. You need to consider the position and what plants to add, as well as any required filtering or aeration systems.

Pond Preparation For Freshwater Fish Farming

Fish is a nutritious food item containing a good amount of protein, omega-3 fatty acids, minerals and other nutrients. It is consumed by the people of India and World on a daily basis. With an increase in demands, the price of fish and fish products are also increasing day by day. So, commercial fish production has established itself as a profit-oriented business. Freshwater fish farming is one of the important fish production systems. It indicates raising and rearing fish in a freshwater system like tanks, ponds and other enclosures in a commercial manner for the purpose of food production. Before starting the fish production, the preparation of the pond is a crucial step which affects the production directly. In this article, we will discuss briefly the pond preparation procedure and how it can help the fish farmers towards better production.

The most important component of the fish farming business is to prepare a pond in a proper way. Without the construction of a well-prepared pond, it is not possible to start or run any fish farming business. The importance of pond preparation is given below.

- Aquatic plants and animals which are harmful to fish are controlled
- Cannibalistic and unwanted fishes are removed
- A healthy environment of the pond is preserved

- Optimum pH for fish production is maintained
- Availability of the feed for the cultured fish is ensured

Types of ponds used in fish farming

Within freshwater fish culture unit, different kinds of pond components are used; they are nursery, rearing, production, segregation and breeding/spawning pool.

The percentage of area covered by these different pond types are given below:

- Nursery pond: 3%
- Rearing pond: 11%
- Production pond: 60%
- Segregation pond: 1%
- Breeding pond: 25%

Nature of different ponds

Nursery ponds: Shallow

Rearing ponds: Moderately deep

Production ponds: Moderately deep

Segregation pond: Moderately deep

Breeding ponds: Moderately deep

Water level (for larger production ponds): 2-3 meters

Preparation of pond

Preliminary or preparation stage

Soil sampling: Before starting other procedures, the soil should be tested. Samples are collected from the bottom of the pond and dike. Generally, pH and organic matter contents are analyzed. pH is important to determine the amount of lime to be treated later. Soil sampling is very important, especially for the new ponds.

- Demudding

One of the most important steps of pond preparation is to "de-mud" the pond, which we wish to prepare. "De-mud" basically is the process of removing mud from the pond which we wish to use. The main purpose of demudding is to make it more suitable for fish farming. Demudding can be done just by removing the mud from the pond, which is the easiest way. Instead of demudding directly, we can go for deepening of our pond which is the best option for larger fishes.

- Pond drying:

The bottom of the pond is dried to remove the unwanted fish species. Drying is done until the soil cracks. Drying also ensures the oxidization of harmful substances and mineralization of organic matters.

- Make the dike of the pond taller

The most common problem of the rainy season for most of the ponds is that flood can carry away fishes of the pond. So, if the pond is located in an area which is closer to the river or stream, then taller embankment or dike is a must. It should be at least 2 to 3 ft higher than the highest level of water in the pond. This can be done very easily and automatically during the time of digging or demudding. Sand removed during de-mudding/digging can be used to make dikes taller. Otherwise, sandbags can be used to make the dikes/embankments taller.

Efficient inlet and outlet system: Efficient inlet and outlet system is very much important for the proper working of the pond system. This mostly comes in the form of a pipe through which water can enter and exit from the system. The inlet system of the pond should be placed slightly higher than the outlet system to ensure maximum water flow.

Proper inlet and outlet system prevent overflow of the pond by taking care of heavy rainfall/slight flood. This is very much helpful for the proper maintenance of water quality.

Controlling harmful aquatic plants and animals: Aquatic weeds and insects both are very much harmful to fish farming ponds as weeds consume almost all nutrients and reduce the amount of oxygen. Their growth should be controlled efficiently so that they cannot create any problem in the pond.

Removing cannibalistic and unwanted fishes: Removal of cannibalistic and unwanted fishes is very much important step in pond preparation. Shol, gozar, boal, taki, etc. are cannibalistic fish and mola, dhela, chanda, pumpti etc. are unwanted fish. They can be removed by drying the pond or by using poison in the pond. Rotenone powder is the best option for this purpose.

- Conditioning the pond

Conditioning is done by application of a layer of lime or calcium hydroxide which is spread over the bottom of the pond for two weeks. It is usually applied during or after the pond drying stage. This removes the acidity of the soil, facilitates biogeochemical cycles and prevents unwanted species.

Liming can be done in three different ways:

- By broadcast over a dried pond which includes the dike walls.
- By mixing with water and spraying over the pond and
- By liming the water flowing into the pond.

Manuring: After 15 days of liming, manuring or fertilization is done in order to facilitate the growth of fish food organisms. Manure can be of organic or chemical nature. The application rate of raw cow dung for stocking pond is 2-3 tonnes/ha. The application rate of poultry manure is 5000 kg/ha. Use of chemical fertilizer depends upon the concentration of phosphorus and nitrogen in the soil and varies accordingly. The standard combination of NPK is 18:10:4 for freshwater ponds.

Conclusion

Fish pond preparation is the basic and first step in freshwater fish farming. Pond preparation is to be done intensively to enhance the fish production of the pond. Without proper preparation of the pond bottom if we start the fish culture technique it will create a huge problem and production will be of poor quality.

In the case of the pond preparation process, good management practices are the basic solution for obtaining better fish yield. Sustainable methods should always be chosen to make pond preparation more suitable for environment-friendly fish farming technique.

Plants and animals both have basic needs in order to survive. Their needs include light, food, air, water, and shelter. Some of these needs may be more or less important to an animal or a plant for survival. Each water quality parameter alone can directly affect the animal health.

Exposure of shrimp and fish to improper levels of dissolved oxygen, ammonia, nitrite or hydrogen sulfide leads to stress and disease. However, in the complex and dynamic environment of aquaculture ponds, water quality parameters also influence each other. Unbalanced levels of temperature and pH can increase the toxicity of ammonia and hydrogen sulfide. Thus, maintaining balanced levels of water quality parameters is fundamental for both the health and growth of culture organisms. It is recommended to monitor and assess water quality parameters on a routine basis.

Printed in Great Britain
by Amazon

25405334R00036